Sourdough Bread

Lady Janét R. Griffin

authorHOUSE®

AuthorHouse™
1663 Liberty Drive
Bloomington, IN 47403
www.authorhouse.com
Phone: 1-800-839-8640

First published by AuthorHouse 1/4/2010

ISBN: 978-1-4490-3805-2 (e)
ISBN: 978-1-4490-3804-5 (sc)

Library of Congress Control Number: 2009910750

Printed in the United States of America
Bloomington, Indiana

This book is printed on acid-free paper.

Sourdough Bread

is
dedicated
to
Mrs. Shirley Dyer
and
as always
my students.

Contents

sourdough bread

let's take a walk
a "screwy" idea
slow steps
holding hands
together.

i don't know you too well
you don't know me
that well
i am the most gorgeous
woman on earth.

i say what i mean
always
mean what i say
most times
hey, i am trying to reach you!

listen to what i say
i know i can do better
let's kiss
and
kiss again
let's have warm sourdough bread
together?

abandon

here animals lived with each another
cackling early mornings
leaving droppings every where
some languished in fields
munching grass all day
chewing cud until round-up time
others squealed in high pitch
swilling slop from dirty wooden troughs
the time was routine.

sun light and morning dew
kissed apple trees and meadow haystacks
in concert they greeted
a new arrival
the time was forever.

the little girl had eyes large, beautiful
yet griped with sparkled fear
apprehension and unformed questions
she was left to stay
no boarding school for her
only a white 'prim and proper' social
worker
unclasped her little black pleading hand
and drove away
the time unforgivable.

and silently he comes

and silently
he comes
soft spoken
but intense
a warrior's friend
with humble tears
like
the long woe
of eagles' cry.

yet his tears
bring mountainous anticipation
longing democratic hope
a new day
and
change so grand
for human hearts everywhere.

little
do we know
his lightly coming
ushers in global love
realms of respect
for
an eagerly awaiting flock!

dedicated to president barack obama

be vigilant ladies

be vigilant ladies
lest our patriarchal societies
battle for dominance
forever.

be vigilant ladies
lest our conditioned inhibitions
are not shed
in time.

be vigilant ladies
lest our spinning wheels
usurp our domestic tranquility
longer than necessary.

be vigilant ladies
lest our prime
may be a time of elusiveness
over night.

be vigilant ladies
lest our daily struggle
for superhuman beauty
is raped every night.

be vigilant ladies
lest our full human rights
return to prudence
again.

be vigilant ladies
lest our sexual thoughts
be divorced from "self"
where we are left
with limpid, wandering eyes.

be vigilant ladies
lest our dawn will come
and it will come
for life's length is less
than life's width.

choose death

choose death
that you may die
when you have
no faith
and believe
life's condition
is beyond
your power to heal.

choose death
that you may die
when you overcome
faith with fear
when you dwell
on appearances
when your vision
stays on imperfection
within yourself
and all people.

choose death
that you may die
when you are ungrateful
and your spirit
is that of a coward
whose reality
turns to pessimism.

choose death
that you may die
when your wholeness
crumbles and
life becomes
a bore
lacking radiance.

choose death
that you may die
when your heart
is broken
and what gives you purpose
has been ripped
from your belly
and dashed
on stones.

choose death
that you may die
when machines
pump the rhythm
of your life
but your feet
are cold
and clammy.

choose death
that you may die
and release
the carbon dioxide
the foliage
who says,
"back up your choice!"

enduring a little better

i can not see
what I write
on the page
but I see
through the haze
of pain and depression
that makes me know
only one step
can be taken
at a time
and although my steps
are small
I am making
advancement
although the pain
is intense
I am enduring
a little better.

expressions of nature

while one speaks
there is utter chaos
a bee sting's
a shark attacks
a tree falls
a volcano erupts
a man dies
a momentary mass
of cyclic happenings
clouding human experience
yet
this is the real world
expressions of nature.

fallen tears

fallen tears

are not lost

they are captured

on the pedals

of time

as shimmering dewdrops

bathing, soothing, caressing

the most fragrant flower

in nature

the rose.

fighting a duel

should there be
brooding of the past
cause
life has been gravely wounded?

should there be
medals offered or refused
just as violently?

or

should there be
hunting and wrestling
with the conscience
for
the present
and
the future
are now
fighting a duel?

forever after

shall we capture in a decade
what we did not in a century?
the words were always there
unconventional in lines
pledging our willingness
capturing our very souls
encouraging us
to leave behind
nothing.

even our illicit love affair
brought inner thoughtful brilliance
and reminder of primitive
never forgotten allure.

we were anything
but average
remember i loved you
as our gravitation toward
clandestine poetry
reached a higher plane
where time was
forever after.

fun and frolic

fun and frolic
swirl you
like a
merry-go-round
but
inevitability
broken dreams
and hopes
cloud the moments
with despair.

fun and frolic
have their moments
the drinks
the ecstasy
the music
but
quiet reveries
are sure to come
rude awakenings
rock reality
no one knows
but you.

ghost

and it came
unknown
its head
was poised
listening
to what
nobody knows
but
it was
with equal authority
nightmarish
as black night
from which
it stumbled
in disbelief
absorbing
every grotesque detail
hearing
every keening sound
that
made its mouth freeze
in
hopeless anguish.

grief ii

grief is slowly
sapping all the
strength from
my body
i can
see my life
ebbing away
each and every moment
as every day pass
before another
what will be
left is a shell
of an individual
who can not
go on with life
filled with NOTHING!

happiness is

happiness is
moments of tranquility
as well as
voices of laughter

past reflections
as well as
present enjoyments

realms of relaxation
as well as
essence of exhilaration

happiness is
within the mind
as well as
within the heart

it rings in a word
it sings in a song
and
it shines in a smile.

happiness is not dispensed

happiness
is not dispensed
in
smooth charm
and
bravado
great or small
leaving only
half-persons
worth NOTHING
but
old bitterness
instead
it is within
as a piece of BLACK coal
embedded deep
in the soul
a dazzling diamond
although
in the rough.

high drama

i have extracted
only what seems
to be the essence
of my character
the year I lived
is unknown
highlights are given
with flamboyant zest
while i fast forward
over the mundane
and
unremarkable periods
yet do I come alive
breathe, move, love
or
do i die
ignobly
the vibrancy
of high drama?

hot icicles

he
was
like hot icicles
sticky with frost
nakedly opulent
and unashamed.

dedicated to skip.

i a woman

i a rose
cannot
a hundred days
bloom.

i a woman
cannot stand
a hundred days
gloom.

i care

weep now
let your tears
mingle with mine
today
they sing of grief
tomorrow
they will massage
our souls
because
i care.

i cry out with joy

i cry out with joy
like the ocean
around the dock
splashing violently
on each jagged rock
yet
i never cease
to find
in my own anger
some source of peace
while i stand
idly mute
in the vast presence
of quietness and strength
to refute
what my own eyes see
and weak body senses
in the loud thunderous
clamor of wind and tide
that
the ocean of life
engulfs me
in waves so wide so deep
in ocean cliffs of love
that
i can cry out with joy.

i have lost

i have lost
much of myself
yet
i still possess
considerable strength.

i must face
new challenges
that will not meltdown
anymore of ME
for forces
shaping the planets
mold my form
determine my destiny.

yet
the march of seasons
the wind and cold
the change of tides
the failure and success
of ME
my crafty enemies
who lurk about ME
as carrion birds
upon a corrugated roof
are contending forces
in my universe.

as i hammer
at my own malleability
endlessly sorting
endlessly discarding
endlessly reshaping
i must resist
the urge
to be smashed
in the human crucible
for there
i can only be
reduced
refined
reworked
into a mere memory.

i lost my balance

at the far edge
of the planet
i walked
with measured steps
there were no
cultivated verdant lawns
but
only rock gardens of depression
glistening in my head below
near the precipice
under bare gnarled branches
hiding human misery
in monumental proportions
shielded from the sobering sun
grouped in great bunches
of pain and grief
yet
the ritual continued
as I walked
soundlessly across the planet
cat walking
ever so silently
noiselessly as always
until
i lost my balance.

it's winter

dewdrops kiss roses
it's spring
red and golden leaves
it's autumn
vacationing crowds gone
it's the last of summer
hearts acquire a velvety shading
ponds shining light
with shimmery ice doing funny things
with paradoxes
capturing skillfully
seasonal emotions
with
a bitter bite
the snow falls
it's winter.

it was love before

it was love before
but nothing
like what it is now
no one knows
but
love lights
my soul from within
like a festival torch
i am helpless
to conceal it
like
i am helpless
to stop my tears.

last goodbye

temporary replacement
is always arriving
like
a painful divorce
uncharacteristically early
unexpected
slightly thin
slightly photogenic
careless
about fidelity
but
savoring each phase
of
illicit adventure
from
the first twinge
of passion
to the last
scary goodbye.

memorial

the sun will light tomorrow
and shine as brightly as before
the world will go on as ever
with one less soul no more.

each day will break in gladness
that sparkles in golden gleams
while birds keep on chirping
in the desert of somber dreams.

silent stars will go on twinkling
till the sunrise by the sea
and a friend of tranquil beauty
shall nevermore be.

midnight will not last forever
in echoes of anguished hearts
there will be a calm reassurance
that fades and then departs.

dedicated to mrs. clarita flores

more advice

should you wish
to travel as a queen
look to SELF
for
marriage is a sink
well-equipped for dish pan hands.

create your own court
be your own court jester
full of kaleidoscopic colors
spinning lace parasols
ankle length evening gowns
with golden hair pins
to pamper coiffure hair
of extraordinary beauty
silhouetting the sky.

no quiet time

there are no quiet days
no quieter evenings
no wonderfully low-key
romantic beginnings
only early morning sounds
serenading to me
a wake-up call
a dog yapping
for my breakfast
a nervous rooster crowing
a greeting for my lost dawn
a wandering cow mooing
insistently for my milk
a pesky woodpecker drilling
my bark for fat insects
all
chasing my waves
competing for my attention.

no longer who i was

death, divorce, despair
came painfully upon me
like bitter waters
and bitter tears
yet
the world
knows me no longer
for
my change is no longer
who i once was
or
who i will be
but
a filament of connection
nurturing amniotic waters
who i am NOW!

no more forever

i serviced you
but
i am not your servant
sometimes life forces me
chattel that i am
to make changes
the soapbox is my medium
i stand erect on wooden platform
chastened
but
classy and cheap.

sometimes
there is another truth
i found you
ignored your drug addiction
your menial employment status
your chauvinistic privilege
but
i sent you packing
i will think of you
no more
forever.

no war of roses

it was
no war of roses
it was
torture
rape
beatings
executions
genocide
and poverty
parading down the street.

compassion stabbed
no one
but
reality of war did.

pain and time

pain makes us self-centered
we hide and cringe
in the bosom of our affliction
and we are too aware of time.

pain gnaws at us
like a vulture
picking at our flesh
before the sun goes down.

pain torments us
and keeps us squirming
with self inside
aching and aching and aching some more.

pain exposes our wound
raw and festering
yearning, longing
for heavenly healing.

but pain and time
play havoc with us
bending us out of shape
until time touches our tenderness
and pain pass away.

prince rising

he was
no creature solitaire
but
a creature
of air and flame
half human
half avian
blazing
across the lives of many
vanquishing
sad windmills
he was a vanishing prince
perhaps
never to reappear.

dedicated to skip

prodigal son

his air was
completely silent
yet watchful
in the
early morning sunshine
he was different
in his
sudden silence
which left
an odd gentleness
unknown
in men
of his stature
tall, muscular, strong
my
prodigal son.

dedicated to my son, patrice antoine
griffin

promise in fantasy

i saw
what i wanted
to see
coming from
sharper focus
the intangible
silhouetted profile
at the lighted doorway
veiled face
in the fog
secreted body
graceful, tall
unmeasured range
of sensual masculinity
hiding a vainly sought
glistening glint
in the eye
i coveted
the grandeur of the scene
in moments
of endearment
i saw
what i wanted
to see
promise in fantasy.

questions

am i
darkening with age
seeing only
the dark seam in life
do i strip
layers off people
a little bit
and find typical emotions
like
anger and jealousy
fear and rage
real burning
destructive desires
all sorts of things
normally associated
with what life really is?
or
am i
willy-nilly
shifting back and forth
sequestered
in my own
personal world of reality
for some
unfathomable reason?

quickly shifting clouds

quickly shifting clouds
rumble gently
smiling on
dozens of glaciers
carving virgin peaks
and whirls of snow
sparkling in the sun
bracing the wind blow
the rugged traveler.

quickly shifting clouds
sudden and treacherous
storming on
silently
without notice
crouching down
covering a deeper
rockier descent
stupefying
the traveler's piercing cry.

reflections ii

variety makes life interesting
but do not get lost
in a sea
of endless possibilities.

push your own rock
up the hill daily
perchance it should
fall at the end of the day
for this insanity will make you sane.

do not become ringed around
with sugar-plum fairies
who dance from every media
for when real life meets you
it will never seem as good.

fulfillment is difficult to find
perhaps, does not exist
but there are no guarantees
so do not complain
should you bark up
the wrong tree.

commitment to life saves us
what we commit to
is not important
but that we make
some commitment
perchance you can not commit
to something big
commit to something small.

the search for perfection
is always a search for SELF
we shall never find it
as long as
we feel inadequate ourselves.

reflections iii

look within
before bearing
accusations against others
for one
who thinks
himself hated
is one
who
easily hates.

entertain less
of what attracts
the attention
of millions
for primitive beliefs
may once more
be confirmed.

be attracted
to what attracts
of the conscience
as well as
the artistic sensibility
for the tension
between the two
speaks
to one's own time.

be calm
in the haste
of emotions
for in its journey
there is
no room for two.

remember when

remember when
mount vesuvius erupted
and buried pompeii and heculaneum?
doomsayers chanted
"zeus punished them!"

remember when
medieval compendium of knowledge
was little more than scientific nonsense?
the earth was considered flat.

remember when
morality stories guiding life's
journey were silly chattering
less suited for the here and now?
only females wore a scarlet letter.

remember when
hatred and bigotry
paralyzed the nation's soul?
black girls could be
re-classified as white
and
all would be well.

remember when
human ignorance was crystal clear?
miracles were miracles
and
apocalypse was a belief
not human progress.

saddest thing

the saddest thing
in the world
is life.

for all
that we hold
is misery.

we mold it
shape it
caress it.

it is mine
nevertheless
it can not
be taken away
AGAIN
but once!

sad tune

don't place a time
on my grief
or shake your head
when you see me weep
but better yet
walk a mile
in my pantaloons
then you may have more empathy
when you hear
my sad tune.

don't ignore me
when you see
the pain in my eye
or ask a silly question
"i wonder why?"
but remember what you see
that darkens my way
may later stalk
and block your path
another day.

so don't sit in judgment
and play god with me
saying i should be
thankful
for what is left me
for life is too short
and over too soon
to fake happiness
from a sad tune.

searching

i noticed the pain
of this headache
it is just another
link to depression
that pulls me
down the road
to self-pity
and more self-pain.

i am tired
of worrying
about the unknown
for the unknown
becomes know
in its own time.

i need strength
self-assurance
and more love
than it takes
to make the world
go round.

but i shall find it
cause I am
searching
one who searches
will ultimately find.

shall i

shall i beam
as the owl
smiling silently
over brief accomplishments?

shall i peck
as the woodpecker
wondering and exploring?

shall i sing
as the robin
musing over millions of melodies?

shall i pray
as the thornbird
loving only who will love in return?
or

shall i see
as the hawk
surveying a more lofty perspective
than other
incisive observers?

shall i speak about life after death?

shall i speak
about life after death
when all around
is bitterness and pain?

shall i exchange
periodic pain
for a lifetime
of dull
chronic pain
when all around
is dreary
a living death?

shall i speak
about life after death
when i'm not living
this one?

shall i speak of this dreary night?

shall i speak of this dreary night
when blackness crowds around me
and keeps me from seeing the
glow of a million stars?

i know they are there
and each one will
eventually light my path
until i find the
NEW ME.

until that time
i shall speak of that dreary night
as i help others
to find their path
to do so will join
my train to the stars
and add steel
to my planet.

shall we

shall we
love those
whose love
does not
change with age?

shall we
relinquish responsibility
for those
who have given
sustenance and life?

shall we
help those
who never ask
for a hand-out?

shall we
diminish the rights
of those
who fought and died
for rights
which are now enjoyable?

shall we
care for those
who were
caregivers?

shall we
enforce
an age discrimination law
for those
who fought gallantly
against age bias?

shall we
invest
in those
who have
proven performance records?

shall we
accept
unfair retirement plans
for those
who have EARNED
the right to retire?

shall we
find solutions
to the frailties
of later life
because to do so
enhance the quality
of ALL life?

shall we
give energy
and
high priority attention
to those
who deserve
reform legislation?

shall we
exempt
apprenticeship programs
for those
who wish to retrain?

shall we
ensure support
for those
who are older
and
those
who plan to grow older?

SHE

SHE
rises
to universal meditation
seizing soliloquies
to echo her soul
through introspective musings
expressed
in grandiose passages
SHE
insinuates herself
through soft crevices
where
acts of pleasure
are
acts of pure expediency
they exists only
as
SHE
exists.

shells of pearls

i searched the shells for pearls
every two years
i found my flesh
five in all
two males, three females
each
seven to nearly ten pounds
of what i wanted
to hold, to dress, to kiss.

they were bundles of
hopes and dreams
but
my story ended
ebbing and flowing as the sea
drowning
my shells and my pearls.

silence reigns supreme

no one was there
no one was likely to come
no one was heard or seen
only the grandeur
of the moment
spoke silently
swishing thoughts of thoughts
bringing
weeping tears
not from grief
but from tears of tender memories
where
silence reigns supreme.

sky of silence

i am
a bare tree
standing upon
the stage of seasons
heavy
with winter snow
in spring
i spread
garments of green
in autumn
i sow seeds in sunlight
and in summer
i raise my branches
and
whisper into
the
sky of silence.

dedicated to my friend, rev. john woodall.

snort of coke

only winged gods
ascend the sky
and leave
worldly montages
of hopelessly unaware
veering beyond comprehension
bantering between
dream and reality
so ironic
so dispiriting
risking death
defying the odds
creating
a curiously dark cluster
of
despair
frustration
failure
with every
snort of coke.

the quintessential prostitute

she has no face
sometimes called fifi
objectified and alluring
as men slather her body
with fifty dollar bills
to bump and grind in sensual gyrations.

she rejects what she wants
giving only what she can control
life is all in her rhythmic routine
where johns lust for her
but never possess an elusive fantasy.

the unattainable slips away
although fragile
marvelously human
her lifestyle is no catalyst of change
it is steeped in the familiar
the social construction
of what is raw, ready
she is
the quintessential prostitute.

there is more time

bugged by soaring luggage bag fees?
it could be worse
airplanes do collide
there is more time
for political sustaining myths.

tune into a realm of reality
it never sinks into violence or compromise
neither black nor white turns gray
there is more time
where neutral observers are no longer
enemies.

make way into that celestial city
destiny date looks better in hollywood
beauty is camouflaged
there is more time
to slip away from the hype.

turn life's turmoil around
offer hospitality; offer nurturance
the homeless still have no homes
there is still time
put it in full motion.

watch what the planets emit
the quirky cocktail won't fix
creationism or evolutionism
there is more time
for sanity to trudge in silence.

search for that zero-sum journey
watch the balance of another's loss
the earth may still seem flat
but
there is more time
to love that stranger.

they are all gone now

they are all gone now
and i
am left
in the night of thousand eyes
but
it is strange
how much my heart
will NEVER forget
their smiles
and
cinnamon hair and eyes.

they are all gone now
and i
am left
with clinging images
of my own flesh
coming and fading
fading and coming
in moments of quiet
in moments
of pain, longing, and loneliness
when an hour
before sleep
comes
too late.

to find a blank sheet

on pages
moving and often tortured
with print saying NOTHING
on pages
black and wet
with automatic outbursts
on pages
purified ruthlessly
with inhibiting imaginative freedom
on pages
terrifyingly threatening
with disenchanted illusions
on pages
vine clinging
with learned weakness and vulgarity
the poet struggles
with rare wanton exception
to find
a blank sheet.

together

together
we can look the world over
and see the charm
of lesser known places
we can bring back
what use to be
like delicate creatures.

together
we can float with electric clouds
with photographic precision
we can dance the dance of purple passion
reigning over mingled bodies.

together
we can sail out to sea
with waves of leering faces
we can twirl the pedals
of erotic flowers
and bring a warm respite
to an autumn love that never died.

but only
together.

tragedy is no less

tragedy is no less
because it is
a familiar trek among many
it is waged, watched
and remembered with horror
on screens of melodrama
played bitchily
in eternal flashbacks
to tempt
the patience of Job.

wake up mister

wake up
wake up mister
we too live on this planet
your seductions have no solace for us
we undress our own beds
we lounge on our own paradise of pleasure
we are free from your
"banging" presence.

wake up
wake up mister
you had thousands of battle-worn years
to break the bough that cradle rocks
to control our choices
from our necks to our emerald toenails
we fall asleep no more
in your hypocritical arms
imprisoned in sorrow's land
where our tears flame
and singe our awakening!

epilogue

My son, Patrice Antoine Griffin, was murdered in 1982. I thought to myself then that the sun would never shine again. I was numb to most of my surroundings, and the usual words of sympathy escaped me all together. Yet, I remember vividly during my darkest days that a colleague and friend of mine, a mother too, approached me, tapped on my shoulders, and said, "I have a son, and I will share him with you."

Sourdough Bread moments are rare indeed. They are moments of empathy, moments of unspoken words, and moments of life transformations. Today, I am so very grateful to Mrs. Shirley Dyer, who has been sharing her son, Mr. Miraculous Dyer, with me.

about the author

Janét R. Griffin, whose professional name is Lady Janét, obtained a B. S. degree from the District of Columbia Teachers College in English and Mathematics, a M. A. degree from Howard University in African American Literature, a Certificate of Advanced Graduate Studies in Supervision and Administration, and a Certificate of Advanced Graduate Studies in Women's Studies. As a professed follower of the philosopher Socrates, and a strong believer that the unexamined life is really not worth living, Lady Janét pursues at least one graduate course every semester from a wide range of disciplines, including philosophy, psychology, education, sociology, fine arts, communication, and women's studies.

Currently, Lady Janét is an English/Study Skills instructor in the Center for Academic Reinforcement, School of Education of Howard University and is a team-teacher in the School of Sociology. She has been an English Lecturer in a number of universities and community colleges in the Washington Metropolitan area, including George Washington University, The University of The District of Columbia, Bowie University, Prince Georges Community College, and Montgomery Junior College.

Lady Janét has traveled extensively throughout the free world, including her favorite destinations: Africa and China. She has remarked often that her active, on-going education, worldly travels, and vast teaching experiences over the years inform and enliven her passion for mentoring students worldwide. New Horizons, an on-campus Howard University student dance organization, is one of her latest role as advisor/mentor. Numerous copies of letters and electronic mail from students all over the world, as well as parents, reveal lively interactions of "keeping in touch" and "thank you for your continued support."

Although Lady Janét is involved actively in a number of hobbies, three have become more than an avocation. Fashion modeling and ballroom dancing are two of them, and poetry writing is the other that she began in high school.

The poems of Lady Janét have been read on WHUR, Howard University Radio, at several social gatherings, at commemorative services, at book clubs, and at poetry readings. The most requested poem, "Do Not Slay My Soul," was read and analyzed by Nikki Giovanni on Morning Break, CBS Television, channel nine.

Lady Janét's poems have been published in numerous periodicals and newspapers, including the Flier, newspaper for Columbia, Maryland; CSP World News, a monthly published in Ottawa, Ontario; and the American Atheist Journal. They have been published also in anthologies: Janus, published by the English Department, Howard University; and American Poetry Anthology, an anthology of contemporary verse. Record, published quarterly by Kappa Delta Pi, an International Honor Society in Education; and Sisters, published by the National Council of Negro Women have each published her poems.

Lady Janét won first place in the poetry contest sponsored by the Middle Atlantic Writer's Association, October 1985, and she has been awarded Certificates of Honorable Mention on numerous occasions from the World of Poetry Contest. Letters of commendation have been received from several renowned writers, including Nikki Giovanni and Maya Angelou.

Sourdough Bread is the tenth published collection of her poems that can be viewed along with Moment in the Sand, and Solitude of Being on www.momentinthesand.com

Other anthologies published previously are Amphony, Volumes I, II, III, Messages From the Veil of Tears, Share the Mystique, Eros and Erotica, and Voices From The River Styx. Each can be viewed on her website: http://shop.ladyjanetgriffin.com

Other contact information can be obtained via emailing jgriffin@howard.edu or janetrobinsongriffin@yahoo.com

www.ingramcontent.com/pod-product-compliance
Lightning Source LLC
Chambersburg PA
CBHW020340290526
45785CB00005B/2113